Creepy Creatures

Snails

Monica Hughes

Heinemann LIBRARY

Little Nippers

www.heinemann.co.uk/library
Visit our website to find out more information about **Heinemann Library** books.

To order:
 Phone 44 (0) 1865 888066
 Send a fax to 44 (0) 1865 314091
 Visit the Heinemann Bookshop at www.heinemann.co.uk/library to browse our catalogue and order online.

First published in Great Britain by Heinemann Library, Halley Court, Jordan Hill, Oxford OX2 8EJ, part of Harcourt Education. Heinemann is a registered trademark of Harcourt Education Ltd.

Designed by Jo Hinton-Malivoire and bigtop, Bicester
Models made by Jo Brooker
Originated by Dot Gradations
Printed by South China Printing Company, Hong Kong/China

ISBN 0 431 16304 9 (hardback)   ISBN 0 431 16309 X (paperback)
06 05 04 03 02   06 05 04 03 02
10 9 8 7 6 5 4 3 2 1   10 9 8 7 6 5 4 3 2 1

British Library Cataloguing in Publication Data
Hughes, Monica
    Snails. - (Creepy creatures)
    1.Snails - pictorial works - Juvenile literature
    I.Title
    594,3'8

Acknowledgements
The Publishers would like to thank the following for permission to reproduce photographs:
Heather Angel p7; Ardea: pp6, 21, John Daniels p19, Steve Hopkin pp12, 22a, 22b, A Weaving p22a; BBC NHU: Juan Manuel Borrero pp4/5, 17; Bruce Coleman: Jane Burton p14; Holt: p22c; Natural Visions: Brian Rogers p16; NHPA: Ant Photo Library p13, Image quest 3D p11, E A Janes p10; Oxford Scientific Films: pp15, 18, K G Vock p20; Robert Harding Picture Library: pp8, 9.

Cover photograph reproduced with permission of Premaphotos/K.Preston-Mapham.

Our thanks to Annie Davy for help in the preparation of this book.

Every effort has been made to contact copyright holders of any material reproduced in this book. Any omissions will be rectified in subsequent printings if notice is given to the Publisher.

Contents

Snails

A snail has a soft **slimy** body and a hard shell.

Looking for snails

You might find snails in the garden after it has been raining.

You might find them
hidden under leaves.

A snail's body

The snail's body is called the foot.

A snail can pull its foot right inside its shell.

A snail's tentacles

A snail has two **long** tentacles
with an eye at each end.
Can you see this
snail's eyes?

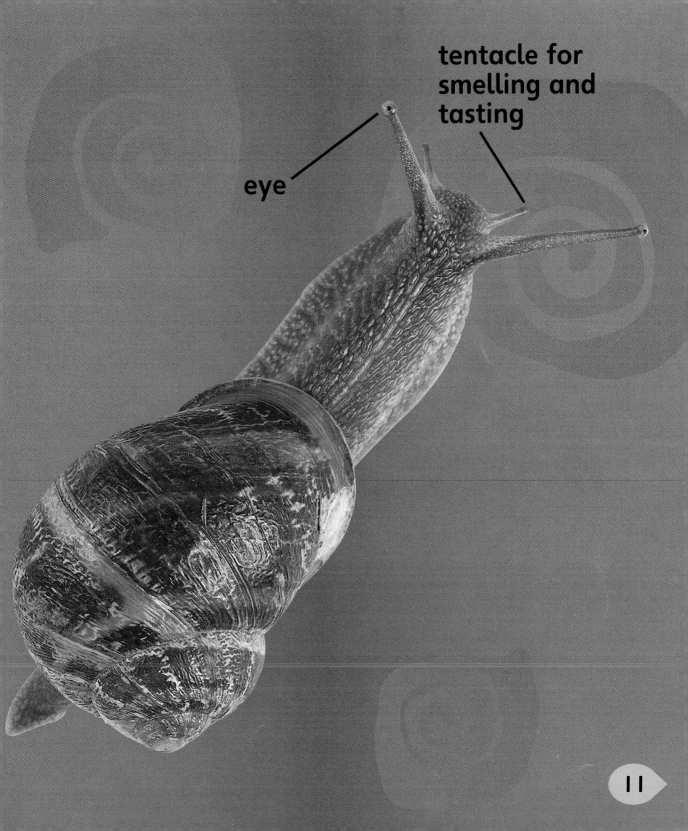

eye

tentacle for smelling and tasting

Snail trails

Snails move very slowly, gliding along on a layer of **slime**.

Snail eggs

When the eggs hatch the tiny snails have a soft shell and body.

Food for snails

Snails eat the leaves and flowers of dead plants.

They also eat young plants.

Snails in danger

When a snail is in danger it goes right inside its shell. Do you think this is a good place to go?

Sometimes it makes foam to
protect it from being attacked.

Snails in winter

Snails sleep
through the winter.

They go right
inside their shells
and seal them
with **slime**.

Types of snails

There are hundreds of different types of snails.

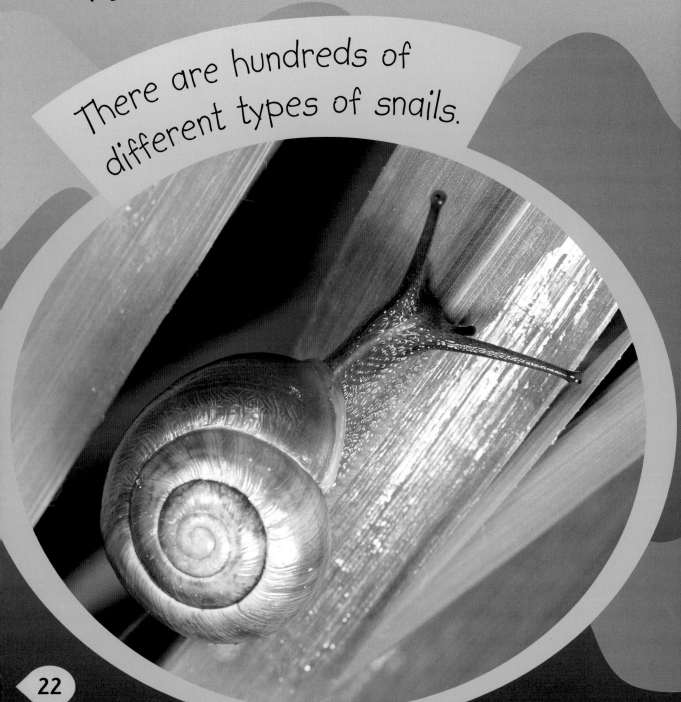

Some are very tiny, others are much **bigger**.

Index

The end

Notes for adults

This series supports the young child's exploration of their learning environment and their knowledge and understanding of their world. The four books when used together will enable comparison of similarities and differences to be made. (NB. Many of the photographs in **Creepy Creatures** show them much larger than life size. The first spread of each title shows the creature at approximately its real life size) The following Early Learning Goals are relevant to the series:
• Find out about, and identify, some features of living things, objects and events that they observe.
• Ask questions about why things happen and how things work.
• Observe, find out about and identify features in the place they live and the natural world.
• Find out about their local environment and talk about those features they like and dislike.

The books will help the child extend their vocabulary, as they will hear new words. Since words are used in context in the book this should enable the young child to gradually incorporate them into their own vocabulary. Some of the words that may be new to them in **Snails** are *tentacles*, *trail* and *protect*.

The following additional information may be of interest:
Snails cannot see very clearly but they can tell the difference between bright and dim light. A snail's mouth is at the front of the underside of the foot. The snail eats by scraping its tongue along the food. Its tongue is covered with hard tiny teeth. It breathes through a hole on the foot near the shell. Snails hatch after about six weeks and garden snails can live for between two and three years. As they age the foot grows and so does the shell with new growth forming at the bottom.

Follow-up activities
The child can record what they have found out about snails by drawing, painting, model-making, tape recording or writing.